P9-DME-235

Cooking with Sunshine

How Plants Make Food

by Ellen Lawrence

Consultants:

Suzy Gazlay, MA
Recipient, Presidential Award for Excellence in Science Teaching

Dr. Robin Wall Kimmerer
Professor of Environmental and Forest Biology
SUNY College of Environmental Science and Forestry, Syracuse, New York

Kimberly Brenneman, PhD
National Institute for Early Education Research, Rutgers University
New Brunswick, New Jersey

BEARPORT PUBLISHING

New York, New York

Credits

Cover, © formiktopus/Shutterstock; 3BL, © windu/Shutterstock and © L_amica/Shutterstock; 3TR, © Madlen/Shutterstock and © aopsan/Shutterstock; 3BR, © Vaclav Volrab/Shutterstock; 4T, © Susan Montgomery/Shutterstock; 4B, © Jacinta/Shutterstock; 5, © Hannamariah/Shutterstock; 6, © Tatiana Popova/Shutterstock and © Olesia Bilkei/Shutterstock; 7L, © Filipe B. Varela/Shutterstock; 7R, © Filipe B. Varela/Shutterstock and © Mayovskyy Andrew/Shutterstock; 8L, © aopsan/Shutterstock; 8R, © Ruby Tuesday Books Ltd.; 9, © Orla/Shutterstock and © creativeoxfoto/Shutterstock; 10, © Sergey Skleznez/Shutterstock; 11, © Power and Syred/Science Photo Library; 12L, © Sailor/Shutterstock; 12R, © Uros Medved/Shutterstock; 13, © Triff/Shutterstock and © Vasilius/Shutterstock; 14–15, © Vaclav Volrab/Shutterstock; 16, © Vasca/Shutterstock; 17, © Vovan/Shutterstock; 18T, © Joy Brown/Shutterstock; 18B, © Elena Butinova/Shutterstock; 19, © Martin Valigursky/Shutterstock; 20, © arnlep/Shutterstock and © Eric Isselée/Shutterstock; 21, © Orla/Shutterstock and © creativedoxfoto/Shutterstock and © Erik Lam/Shutterstock and © Ljupco Smokovski/Shutterstock and © maridav/Shutterstock; 22, © Image Source/Superstock; 23TL, © Artur Synenko/Shutterstock; 23TC, © Gunnar Pippel/Shutterstock; 23TR, © Chiyacat/Shutterstock; 23BL, © Orla/Shutterstock; 23BC, © Vaclav Volrab/Shutterstock; 23BR, © Pongphan.R.

Publisher: Kenn Goin
Editorial Director: Adam Siegel
Creative Director: Spencer Brinker
Design: Elaine Wilkinson
Photo Researcher: Ruby Tuesday Books Ltd

Library of Congress Cataloging-in-Publication Data

Lawrence, Ellen, 1967–
   Cooking with sunshine : how plants make food / by Ellen Lawrence.
      p. cm. — (Plant-ology series)
   Audience: 6–9.
   Includes bibliographical references and index.
   ISBN 978-1-61772-586-9 (library binding) — ISBN 1-61772-586-2 (library binding)
   1. Plants—Development—Juvenile literature. 2. Plant cells and tissues—Growth—Juvenile literature. 3. Photosynthesis—Juvenile literature. I. Title. II. Title: How plants make food.
   QK731.L39 2013
   572'.46—dc23

                                          2012012183

For more information, write to Bearport Publishing Company, Inc., 45 West 21st Street, Suite 3B, New York, New York 10010. Printed in the United States of America.

10 9 8 7 6 5 4 3 2 1

Contents

It's Feeding Time!

On a sunny afternoon, animals in a park are busy looking for food.

A squirrel scampers in the grass eating seeds.

Caterpillars wriggle from plant to plant looking for juicy leaves to munch on.

The animals aren't the only ones feeding, however.

The park's plants are also getting food—without even moving from place to place.

caterpillar

squirrel

Plants come in many different shapes and sizes. A tree is a very big plant. A grassy lawn is made up of thousands of small grass plants.

How do you think plants get food?

Roots, Stems, and Leaves

To grow and live, plants make their own food using their **roots**, stems, and leaves.

Roots are the part of a plant that grows down into the soil.

The stems of a plant connect the roots to its leaves.

Roots, stems, and leaves all have jobs to do when it's time to make food.

In a notebook draw a picture of a plant. Add these labels to your drawing:
• roots • stem • leaf

soil

stem

leaves

roots

flower

flower

Many plants grow flowers. Flowers don't help plants make their food. They help them make seeds that can grow into new plants.

The Roots and Stems Get to Work

To make food, one of the things plants need is water.

Plants use their roots to take in water from the soil.

The water travels from the roots up a plant's main stem.

It then moves through the plant's thinner stems to the leaves.

Finally, the water spreads through the leaves inside tiny tubes, called veins.

veins

before:

after:

How does water move through a plant? Put half an inch (1.3 cm) of water into a glass and add a teaspoon (5 ml) of blue food coloring. Then take a celery stalk with leaves and cut an inch (2.5 cm) off the bottom end. Place the cut end of the stalk in the blue water. You will see the celery change color as the blue water moves up the stalk.

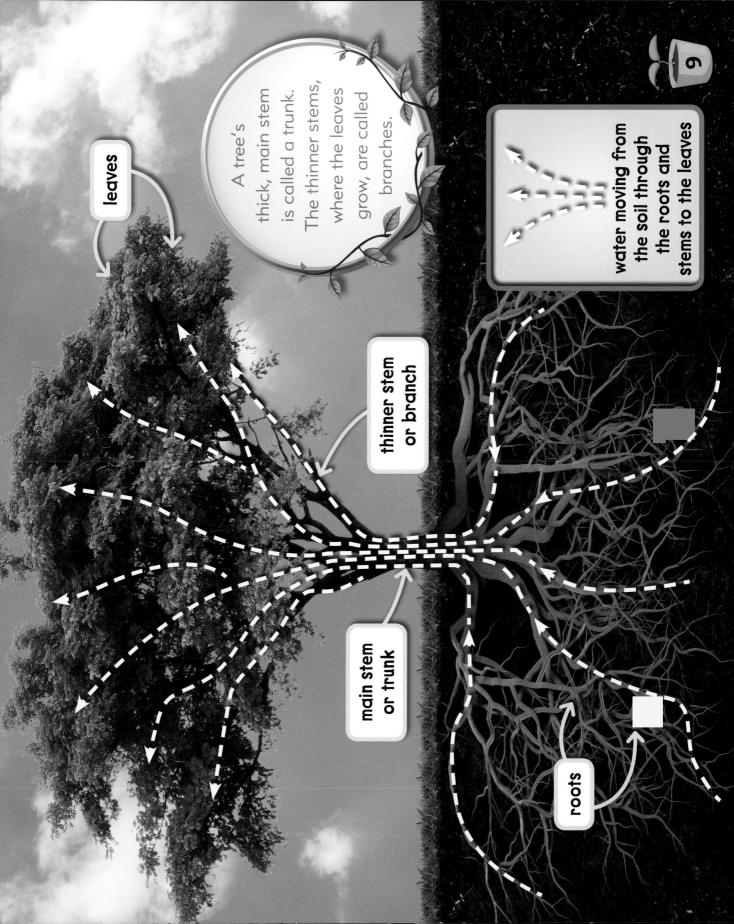

leaves

A tree's thick, main stem is called a trunk. The thinner stems, where the leaves grow, are called branches.

thinner stem or branch

main stem or trunk

roots

water moving from the soil through the roots and stems to the leaves

The Leaves Get to Work

Plants also need a **gas** from the air to make their food.

They collect this gas, called carbon dioxide, using their leaves.

Carbon dioxide enters a plant's leaves through tiny holes.

rose leaf

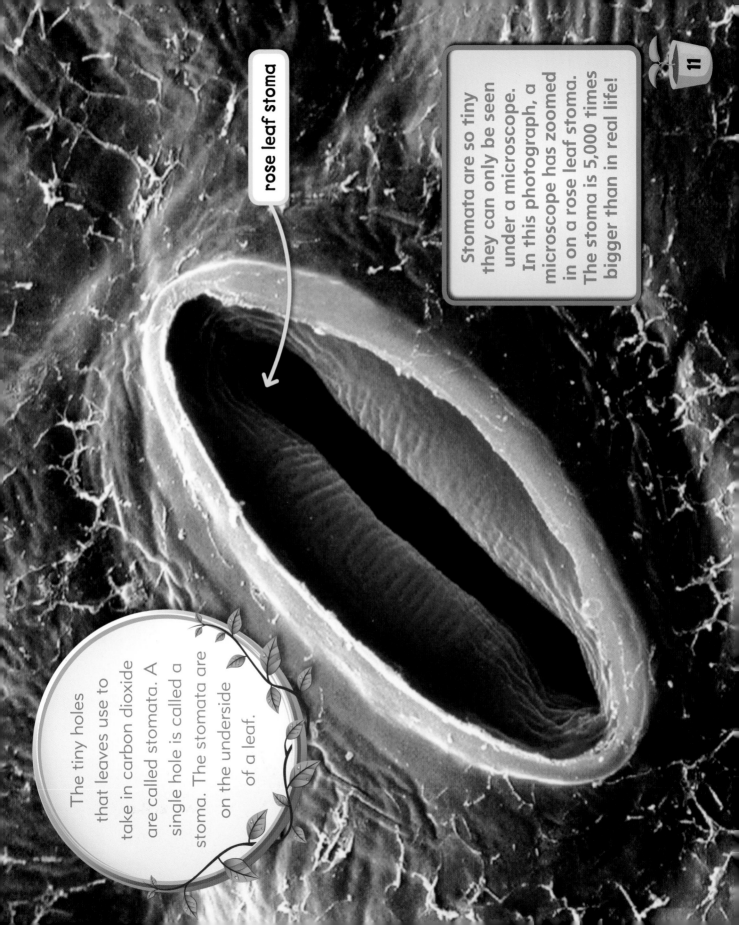

rose leaf stoma

Stomata are so tiny they can only be seen under a microscope. In this photograph, a microscope has zoomed in on a rose leaf stoma. The stoma is 5,000 times bigger than in real life!

The tiny holes that leaves use to take in carbon dioxide are called stomata. A single hole is called a stoma. The stomata are on the underside of a leaf.

Soaking Up Sunshine

The final thing that plants need to make their food is sunlight.

A plant soaks up sunlight using its leaves. When a plant has water, carbon dioxide, and sunlight, it has everything it needs to get cooking!

Leaves can be big, small, long, round, shiny, and even prickly. No matter how they look, all leaves hold water, collect carbon dioxide, and soak up sunlight.

Go on a leaf hunt and try to find as many different sizes and shapes of leaves as you can. Look for the veins. You might need to use a magnifying glass to see some of them.

Cooking with Sunshine

Inside their leaves, plants use sunlight to turn water and carbon dioxide into a sugary food.

This process is called **photosynthesis.**

The food a plant makes is not the same as the sugar that people use to make cakes and other sweet foods.

It's a kind of sugar that plants use for **energy** and to help them grow.

The word "photo" means "light." The word "synthesis" means "putting together." So photosynthesis means "putting together with light."

Cooking Green

Photosynthesis takes place in a plant's leaves with the help of a substance called **chlorophyll**.

Chlorophyll gives plants their green color. It also traps the energy in sunlight.

Chlorophyll uses that energy to make photosynthesis happen in the plant's leaves.

In addition to helping a plant make food, sunlight helps a plant make chlorophyll in its leaves.

Amazing Plants

During photosynthesis, plants don't just make their food.

Something else amazing happens!

Plants make a gas called oxygen.

They give off the oxygen from their leaves.

People and animals need this gas to breathe.

Without oxygen from plants, people and animals would die.

People can't see it happening but all around them plants are making oxygen—from little houseplants on windowsills to grass and tall trees in backyards.

Plants don't only help people by making oxygen. Plants also give people food. What plants have you eaten in the past week?

(There are some ideas to help you on page 24.)

People and Animals Need Plants!

Plants grow and live by making food from water, carbon dioxide, and sunlight.

As they make food, they give off oxygen. Humans and animals need oxygen to breathe.

Many plants could survive on Earth without people and animals.

Without plants, however, people and animals wouldn't have the oxygen they need to live.

Plants get energy from the food they make. To stay healthy, they also need **nutrients** from the soil. They take in nutrients through their roots.

Photosynthesis in Action

Sunlight turns water and carbon dioxide into food inside the leaves.

As the leaves make food, oxygen that people and animals need to breathe is given off.

A plant's leaves take in carbon dioxide from the air.

A plant takes in water through its roots and stores it in its leaves.

Science Lab

Sunlight Experiment

A plant needs sunlight to make both its food and the green chlorophyll in its leaves.

What happens when a plant doesn't get enough sunlight?

To find out, take two potted plants of the same kind that have green leaves.

Place one plant in a sunny place and the other in a dark closet.

Water the plants to keep their soil moist. (Give them both the same amount of water.)

Compare your plants every three or four days.

What do you notice happening? (You can find out what will happen in this experiment on page 24.)

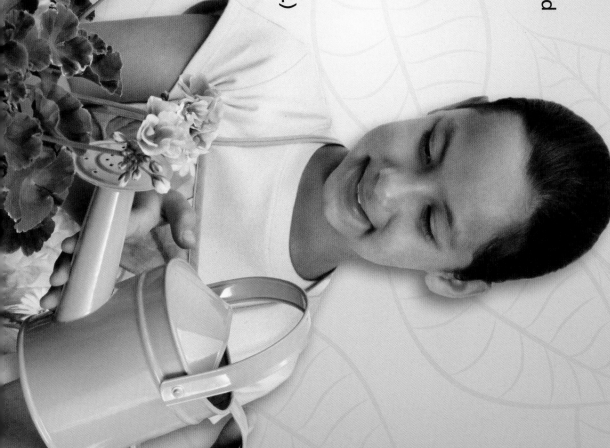

Science Words

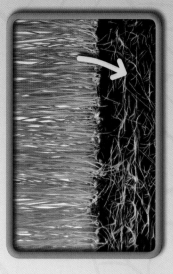

chlorophyll (KLOR-uh-fil) the substance in leaves that traps sunlight and uses it to make a plant's food; it gives the plant its green color

energy (EN-ur-jee) the power needed by all living things to grow, develop, and stay alive

gas (GASS) matter that floats in air and is neither a liquid nor a solid; most gases, such as carbon dioxide, are invisible

nutrients (NOO-tree-uhnts) substances that plants get from the soil, such as nitrogen, which a plant needs to grow leaves and be healthy

photosynthesis (foh-tuh-SIN-thuh-siss) the making of food by plants using water, carbon dioxide, and sunlight

roots (ROOTS) underground parts of plants that take in water and nutrients from the soil; roots spread out in the soil to hold a plant in place

Index

Read More

Bang, Molly, and Penny Chisholm. *Living Sunlight: How Plants Bring the Earth to Life.* New York: Scholastic (2009).

Blackaby, Susan. *Catching Sunlight: A Book About Leaves (Growing Things).* Minneapolis, MN: Capstone (2003).

Kalman, Bobbie. *Plants Are Living Things (Introducing Living Things).* New York: Crabtree (2008).

Learn More Online

To learn more about photosynthesis, visit www.bearportpublishing.com/Plant-ology

About the Author

Ellen Lawrence lives in the United Kingdom. Her favorite books to write are those about nature and animals. In fact, the first book Ellen bought for herself, when she was six years old, was the story of a gorilla named Patty Cake that was born in New York's Central Park Zoo.

Answers

Page 19: All fruits and vegetables come from plants. Bread, cookies, and cereal are made from plants such as corn and wheat. These plants are types of grass, called grains.

Page 22: The plant in the closet will not look as healthy as the other plant. That's because it cannot make food without sunlight. Also, its leaves may start to look pale because it needs sunlight to make green chlorophyll. Be patient, though! It may be several weeks before you see these changes happen.